Original title:
Forest Fables and Farce

Copyright © 2025 Creative Arts Management OÜ
All rights reserved.

Author: Arabella Whitmore
ISBN HARDBACK: 978-1-80567-267-8
ISBN PAPERBACK: 978-1-80567-566-2

The Trickling Stream of Stories

In a glade where whispers sing,
A squirrel dons a tiny ring.
He claims to be the forest's king,
But stumbles when the bluebirds fling.

The stream flows with a glint and laugh,
As frogs wiggle in a silly bath.
A turtle tells a joke by half,
While fish dance—oh, what a gaff!

The Owl's Wise Refrain

An owl hoots with a wink so sly,
Telling tales that twist and fly.
He tells us all the reasons why,
A cat tried to reach the pie up high.

With wisdom perched upon a branch,
He winks and stirs a tiny ranch.
The mice hold a merry little dance,
While dreams of cheese give them a chance.

Revelry beneath the Starlit Boughs

The night is bright, the stars are bold,
With critters gathered, stories told.
A raccoon juggles shiny gold,
A tale of how it all enfold.

The fireflies glow in rhythm fair,
As mischief brews in the cool night air.
A badger's hat, a curious bear,
Becomes a crown, beyond compare.

Fables Written in the Underbrush

In the thicket where secrets thrive,
A hedgehog learns to dance and jive.
With prickly shoes, she comes alive,
The whole caboodle starts to dive.

A green gecko humors all around,
With silly stories, he's renowned.
His lizard laugh is oddly sound,
As joy erupts from underground.

The Squirrel's Secret Scheme

In the tallest oak, a squirrel aims high,
Collecting acorns with a twinkle in eye.
He plots and he schemes with a joyful dance,
Wants to share meals, if the friends take a chance.

But the robins, distracted, chirp on too loud,
While the wise old owl snoozes, swathed in a cloud.
Yet the joke's on the squirrel, his stash goes to waste,
For the wind takes his acorns, no food in the haste.

The Dreaming Grove's Serenade.

In a grove where dreams weave, the moon sings at night,
Where the rabbits explore with their dancing delight.
A bear with a banjo plays tunes to the trees,
Tickling their branches with whimsical breeze.

The raccoons join in, with a tambourine sound,
While the fox strums a guitar, so crafty and round.
They laugh at the shadows, the melodies swirl,
In this comedy patch where dreams freely twirl.

Whispers of the Wildwood

In the twilight of twilight, where whispers abound,
The chipmunk recites tales that nobody found.
With a flourish and spin, he juggles sweet nuts,
While the hedgehog snickers, just shaking his guts.

The shadows grow longer, yet laughter stays bright,
As the fireflies join in, a flickering light.
The breeze tells a story, just tickles the air,
As crickets jump in with their musical flair.

Enchanted Echoes

Near a stream that giggles, the trees toss their heads,
Mice whisper in secrets beneath cozy beds.
A crow with a quip flies like a smart ace,
Making jokes with the frogs in the muddy embrace.

The wind carries tales from the flowered crust,
As the wallabies laugh, condensing the dust.
In this wondrous hush, all the creatures embrace,
Bound by the humor of this magical place.

Legends Crafted by the Wind

A whisper tickles branches high,
As squirrels plot a pie up in the sky.
Rabbits draft their plans so grand,
While owls hoot wise, with jesting hand.

The breeze spins tales like cotton candy,
Of mushrooms dancing, funny and dandy.
A wily fox runs off with a shoe,
Singing songs of mischief, just for a few.

The Caper of the Curious Crickets

Crickets chirp, a band in flight,
Bouncing tunes from day to night.
One lost his bow, what a sight!
They laughed so hard, they took to flight.

Underneath a moon so bright,
Grass blades sway, a joyful plight.
They spin around in leaps and hops,
As fireflies dance and music pops.

Tales of the Timber Troll

A troll with a laugh, wide as a tree,
Tripped on a root, oh, silly he!
His nose was quite long, a curious sight,
He sneezed and sent acorns flying in fright.

With beetles as friends, they plot and scheme,
To bake a pie, or so it would seem.
But flour flew high, a doughy mess,
Leaving them covered, in pure humorous stress.

The Paradox of the Stubborn Cedar

A cedar stood firm, never to bend,
Claiming wisdom with no need to tend.
But when a woodpecker knocked on wood,
The rhythm he made was quite understood.

The tree could not dance, nor could it sway,
Yet giggled at branches, swaying away.
Rooted in place, but fancied the jest,
In the shade of its leaves, laughter was best.

Tales Beneath the Canopy

In a glen where tales unfold,
The squirrels plot, both brave and bold.
They gather nuts for their grand feast,
While bickering like an ancient beast.

A wise old owl, with spectacles clear,
Watches the chaos, sipping his beer.
"Oh, the mischief of these little fools!"
He chuckles softly, breaking the rules.

Mischief Among the Moss

Beneath thick moss, a rabbit danced,
In muddy shoes, he took a chance.
A turtle joined with a clumsy spin,
As the laughter rose, they forgot to win.

A fox bartered lies for a carrot cake,
Swapping the truth for the silliest sake.
With giggles echoing through the trees,
They formed a band, playing tunes with ease.

Secrets of the Sylvan Shadows

In shadows where the secrets hide,
A raccoon crept with a cheeky stride.
He stole some berries, oh what a sight,
As birds squawked loud, taking flight.

A breeze tickled branches, secrets flew,
While the whispering leaves shared gossip too.
Everyone laughed at the squirrel's new hat,
Stitched from a sock, how silly is that?

The Trickster's Grove

In the grove where the mischief thrives,
Badger rolls in the mud, he jives.
A raccoon joins with his every quirk,
Turning this prank into pure work.

With acorns as bombs, they launch into games,
While frogs croak out their silly names.
Even the nightingale starts to hum,
And joins this ruckus—you'll hear the drum!

Hooting Hilarity in the Hollow

In the hollow where the owls dwell,
Hoops and hollers cast a spell.
They dance on branches, wings aflutter,
While squirrels giggle, making a stutter.

With acorns tossed like little bombs,
The laughter echoes, and it calms.
Rabbits join with a playful bounce,
Each leap a chuckle, each twist a pounce.

The moonlight beams, a spotlight bright,
On critters cavorting beneath the night.
The wise old owl starts to sway,
With each silly jig, the world's at play.

In the hollow, laughter reigns,
No one but nature holds the reins.
In this jovial, raucous spot,
Joy beams out, a merry dot.

The Mirthful Moths

By the lamp, they flitter and flap,
The moths come calling, what a trap!
With wings that shimmer, they put on shows,
Spinning silly tales in graceful throws.

They bump and swirl, a comic flight,
Crashing and laughing to their delight.
Each flip a giggle, each spin a cheer,
In the glow of moonlight, they disappear.

In blooms of night, they hold their dance,
A merry meeting, a whimsical chance.
They twist with glee, like leaves in a breeze,
The moths of mirth bring everyone to knees.

A flash of color, a soft little thud,
In their jesting way, they spark pure flood.
And when dawn creeps, the laughter fades,
Yet in the dark, the joy cascades.

Marvels of the Mossy Knoll

On the knoll, so green and round,
Where laughter sprouts from the ground.
The frogs compose a jolly tune,
Singing to stars and the mischievous moon.

A hedgehog joins in with a goofy grin,
Rolling around, he jumps right in.
Together they shake the morning dew,
Each giggle sparkles like drops anew.

Beneath a toadstool, a party brews,
With fireflies buzzing, a lively fuse.
Their games unfold, a playful spree,
Comic capers for all to see.

The mossy knoll, a stage of cheer,
Where antics abound and fun draws near.
In the realm of green, where laughter's grown,
Mirth is the harvest, joy is sown.

The Sprite's Silly Story

In a glade where sprites reside,
Lives a fellow, full of pride.
With mischief twinkling in his eye,
He spins tall tales as days go by.

One day he claimed, with glee ablaze,
That he could float for all his days.
But as he tried to take to air,
He landed plop in a fairy's hair.

The fairy laughed and jiggled too,
Joined in the fun, not just a few.
They'd leap and tumble, giggles galore,
Their frolic echoing from the forest floor.

With every tale, a jest revealed,
Sprightly laughter, joy unsealed.
The sprite's silly ways bring room to cheer,
Forever echoing, drawing near.

The Gnome's Guffaw

In the shade of mushrooms bright,
Gnomes gather with sheer delight.
Their hats are crooked, smiles wide,
They laugh with squirrels who take a ride.

With tiny feet, they skip and prance,
In a silly jig, they twirl and dance.
A chipmunk joins, their nimble mate,
And soon the laughter will not abate.

They share a pie, a berry blend,
In every crumb, a giggle bends.
A faerie drops a flying jest,
The gnomes erupt, they can't digest!

As dusk descends, the joy ignites,
With oddball tales beneath the lights.
In this realm so blissfully daft,
Every chuckle is a crafty craft.

Whimsy in the Wilderness

A rabbit dons a dandy hat,
While otters giggle, sly and fat.
They stage a race, a merry show,
With acorns scattered all in a row.

The tortoise shouts, "You'll lose for sure!"
But laughter wins, it's pure, demure.
A fox steps in with tricks so sly,
This dance of jest, oh me, oh my!

Beneath the trees, they jump and cheer,
Whimsy's theme, the laughter clear.
The punchline lands like rain from skies,
In every corner, funny surprise.

As night falls down, the giggles fade,
But dreams of laughter, still remade.
Tomorrow brings more silly sights,
In wild, enchanting, playful nights.

The Bard of the Bark

A bard with twigs woven for hair,
Sings to the animals everywhere.
His song is strange, with babbling flow,
The critters listen, putting on a show.

With each tune, a giggle burst,
As porcupines roll in silly thirst.
The owl hoots in a comical tone,
In the glen, it's a laughter zone.

A dance breaks out, and bugs take flight,
Spreading joy in the fading light.
The bard keeps singing, tunes odd and bright,
While hedgehogs join in, what a sight!

With echoes now of joyful cheers,
The forest flourishes, banishing fears.
In every corner, the laughs abide,
A merry bard — our goofy guide!

Pantomime Beneath Pine

Upon the stage of roots and stone,
A troupe performs, in glee alone.
With gestures grand, and faces bright,
They prance and leap, a comical sight.

A bear pretends to bake a cake,
While birds assist, and giggles shake.
The lightest joke, the silliest plan,
Leaves everyone rolling, oh what a clan!

As pine trees sway, they steal the scene,
With echoes of laughter, so unforeseen.
The forest cheers, their hearts ablaze,
In pantomime plays that daze and amaze.

As moonlight glows on laughter's trail,
Actors bow, though some may fail.
In whimsical mirth, the night resounds,
With joy that wraps the ground that surrounds.

Woodland Whispers of Wit

In the shade of the giant oak,
Squirrels share their nutty jokes,
A badger giggles, quite the bloke,
As rabbits snort at silly pokes.

The owl wears glasses, quite the sight,
Calling meetings late at night,
"Who's hooting now?" they all delight,
With feathery friends in a feathered fight.

A fox in socks starts up a dance,
While hedgehogs join in, taking a chance,
They twirl and whirl, a spiky prance,
And tumble down, all in a trance.

With laughter bubbling under trees,
The whispers float upon the breeze,
Creatures chuckling, minds at ease,
In this silly place where joy won't freeze.

Eccentricity in the Elders

Grandpa tortoise tells the tale,
Of youthful days on a breezy trail,
But frogs croak loud and start to wail,
"Your stories are long, we simply pale!"

A wise old crow with mismatched socks,
Plays chess with a squirrel and calls out shocks,
"Your moves are nuts, like all your stocks!"
As laughter echoes, the humor rocks.

The rabbits gather, with ears so bright,
To hear the owls mock a moonlit flight,
They conjure up shadows in the night,
While a mime chirps softly, quite a sight!

Embracing quirks, the old and young,
Life's comedies forever spun,
In every laugh, a tale is sprung,
In this wild world, joy is well sung.

Fables of the Fluttering Foliage

Leaves danced in the breeze, quite a sight,
A squirrel wore glasses, thinking it bright.
He read all the signs, upside down too,
Claiming the oak was a wise guru.

The branches giggled with every sway,
As acorns rolled off, joining the play.
The wind whispered secrets, quite absurd,
While mushrooms debated, all undeterred.

A rabbit in boots hopped with great flair,
Challenging vines to a race in the air.
The daisies clapped, cheering his speed,
While the snails took bets, feeling quite freed.

At dusk, the trees gathered for a chat,
Discussing the antics of the old bat.
With shadows growing and laughter so loud,
They swayed like dancers, in a leafy crowd.

Capers of the Coyotes

Under the moonlight, coyotes pranced,
In hats and capes, they waltzed and danced.
Each step a joke, every twirl a pun,
A scene that left the stars stunned, all but one.

One wise old coyote, wrapped in a scarf,
Told jokes 'bout rabbits that made the pack laugh.
With tales of mishaps like slipping on ice,
They rolled in the dirt, oh what a nice slice!

They howled at the moon, a comedic tune,
Echoed by crickets, a merry festoon.
With tails intertwined, they formed a conga,
Leaving behind tales that would surely prolong a.

The sun peeked in, the night came to rest,
Yet laughter lingered, it felt like a jest.
With dreams of tomorrow intertwined in their song,
These capering coyotes knew they belonged.

Raucous Rhymes of the Reeds

In the marshy thicket, the reeds made a fuss,
Playing hopscotch all day, what a raucous plus!
Each stalk a storyteller, weaving their tale,
While frogs in tuxedos danced without fail.

A wind came by, tickling every strand,
As dragonflies giggled, flying hand in hand.
The chorus of crickets clapped out of tune,
Confused, they looked up, 'Is that a balloon?'

Then came a heron with elegant grace,
Attempting ballet, falling flat on his face.
The reeds erupted, their laughter so grand,
While the heron stood up, saying, "Is this my land?"

As twilight descended, again they all sang,
In a raucous assembly, the reeds really sprang.
With tales spun from laughter and dreams that they'd weave,
The night held their secrets, no one would believe.

The Raven's Riddle

A raven sat high, on a branch so stout,
Croaking some riddles, trying to shout.
"Why did the crow fly south on a whim?
Because the sky said, 'Don't come, it's brimmed!'

With feathers askew, he cackled with glee,
As all the pigeons gathered to see.
"Here's one for you, fluffs of white fluff,
What's the best trick when the going gets tough?"

The group stood puzzled, not a clue in sight,
Until one brave dove quipped, "Let's just take flight!"
And off they did go, on wings spread wide,
With laughter echoing, oh what a ride!

As dusk cast a spell, and shadows did play,
The raven just winked, "I'll riddle another day."
For soon they'll convene once more at the crest,
In a game of wise crows, where jesting is best.

Fables Woven of Vines

Once a squirrel stole a hat,
A rabbit said, "That's quite a spat!"
They chased him 'round with lots of cheer,
While birds just laughed from branches near.

A wise old owl gave a wink,
"In mischief, there's more than we think!"
The forest giggled with delight,
As antics echoed through the night.

Moonlit Mischief

The raccoons planned a grand parade,
With shiny pots and forks displayed.
The moon grinned down at their great feat,
As they danced on paws, oh so fleet!

A fox in shades tried to DJ,
While badgers joined, the night to sway.
Laughter twinkled in the trees,
As mischief hummed upon the breeze.

The Dance of the Dappled Light

Sunbeams flicker, tease the ground,
While leaves spin, whirl, without a sound.
A hedgehog twirled with glee, oh my!
His little feet looked quite sly!

Beneath the shade, the shadows play,
As chipmunks jump both night and day.
They twirled in patterns, wild and bright,
Celebrating without a fright.

Ramblings of the Rooted Souls

The trees recounted tales so bold,
Of pranks and jests from days of old.
"Remember when the breeze did blow,
And we saw a snail put on a show?"

With roots entwined, they shared a smile,
While ferns danced softly all the while.
The laughter rang through sap and bark,
Echoing tales till it was dark.

Folklore of the Woodland Spirits

In the glade where squirrels dance,
A hare tells tales of lost romance.
The owls hoot in laughter's sound,
As mischief weaves its merry round.

Trees gossip with a gentle sway,
About the fox who lost his way.
He wore a hat too large, you see,
And tripped on roots, oh what a spree!

Mice hold court on mossy thrones,
Debating acorns, sticks, and stones.
Wise raccoons chuckle at the show,
While peeking from their hiding low.

And fireflies flicker like old jesters,
Enticing dreams, the night investors.
In the heart of twilight's cheer,
The woodland spirits draw near.

Comedy in the Canopy

Up above, the branches sway,
Where birds sing songs in playful sway.
A parrot jesters to the crowd,
With jokes that make them laugh aloud.

A sloth on high plays peek-a-boo,
While monkeys pull their pranks anew.
The toucan beaks just quirk and tease,
As laughter dances on the breeze.

Gnarled roots within the trees
Play tricks on travelers with ease.
One stumbled on a nutty rhyme,
Declaring it the silliest time!

With foliage bright and visions grand,
Every creature lends a hand.
In this laughter-filled array,
Nature sings in a joyous play.

Riddles of the Rustic Realm

In a glen where shadows tease,
A badger writes his quirkiest pleas.
He scribbles jokes on clumps of moss,
While hedgehogs giggle, oh what a toss!

The daisies chuckle, the grass joins in,
As goats skip by with mischief's grin.
"What smells like cheese yet grows on trees?"
The riddle flies on a whispery breeze.

A curious owl hoots, "What am I?"
While squirrels munch, and branches sigh.
The moon rolls in, a silver prize,
Reflecting laughter in playful skies.

So gather round, ye merry souls,
Join the dance as the night unfolds.
In this realm of rustic delight,
Every riddle sparks pure light.

Chasing Shadows Among the Branches

Shadows flit with a jolly jive,
While zealous critters try to thrive.
A raccoon prances in glee and style,
With every twist, he adds to the pile.

Down below, the turtles race,
Belly flops on the grassy base.
"Speedy Turt, what's your plan?"
"We'll win, just give me a hand!"

Above, the crows cackle with glee,
Spreading tales of who fell from a tree.
"I swear I saw him trip on air!"
They tease the breeze, a cheeky flare.

In the midst of nature's fun,
Every game has just begun.
Beneath the leaves, laughter grows,
Chasing shadows, the joy just flows.

Chronicles of the Ancient Oaks

Once stood a tree with a crooked grin,
It told silly tales of the wind's soft spin.
The acorns laughed, rolled down in delight,
While squirrels made faces in the moon's gentle light.

Beneath its branches, a party would start,
With raccoons dancing, they were quite the art.
An owl named Barnaby hooted with flair,
While fireflies twinkled in the cool evening air.

Leaves rustled secrets, the roots shared a jest,
A gathering of giggles, it simply was best.
As laughter echoed through trees all around,
The night wore a coat of giggles profound.

And so in this grove, where tales never tire,
The ancient oak stood, a comedic sire.
With stories aplenty that never grew old,
Each leaf held a memory, ready to unfold.

Revels of the Underbrush

In the thickets below, mischief was rife,
With rabbits and hedgehogs bringing much strife.
They organized games, and debates began,
Who could hop highest or run faster than a man?

A badger jumped in, all covered in mud,
Claiming he'd win, quite sure of his thud.
But turtles, quite clever, just laughed with glee,
For they knew slow and steady could make them all flee.

The bushes would shake, with giggles they'd burst,
Every creature out there felt humor was first.
Even the worms joined in with a wiggle,
They twisted their bodies, making all giggle.

They feasted on berries, spun tales full of glee,
As the moon shone bright, they danced carefree.
In the underbrush merry, where laughter was found,
Gives proof that the happiest creatures abound!

The Squirrel's Silly Saga

There once was a squirrel, named Timmy McChew,
Whose acorn collection was bigger than blue.
He'd stash them in holes and forget where they lay,
Then search for his treasures throughout the long day.

When winter arrived and snow covered ground,
Timmy sat puzzled, his acorns unfound.
He scampered around, in a fluffy black hat,
Chasing a shadow, thinking it was his snack.

His friends came to help, but the vision was bleak,
For finding those acorns, they all felt quite weak.
Yet through all the chaos, they snickered and laughed,
Creating the kind of fun only friends could draft.

Eventually, they found him, quite stuck in a tree,
With a branch as his seat, and he shouted with glee.
"Next time I'll remember!" he promised, with flair,
But he'd soon forget, and we knew he wouldn't care.

Mirages in the Thicket

In a glade full of shadows and sparkles quite bright,
Rumors of treasures would dance through the night.
A fox with a smirk spread stories so grand,
That jeweled carrots lay buried in sand.

The rabbits were fooled, they dug with great might,
Only to find some old roots quite a sight.
With laughter aloud, they declared it a hoax,
And soon all the forest rang out with their jokes.

Dancing around, with sticks in their paws,
The creatures rejoiced without any cause.
The mirage of treasures was pure, silly fun,
An adventure unwound under each rising sun.

So whenever you think that the grass is more green,
Remember this tale, for it's not always seen.
For in every thicket where laughter takes flight,
Mirages can sparkle, bringing joy to the night.

Harmonies of Hoots and Laughter

In the moonlight, owls take flight,
Chasing shadows, such a sight.
With giggles dancing on the breeze,
Whispering secrets past the trees.

Squirrels in coats of nutty hues,
Playing tag and telling news.
They leap and bound, with no care,
Leaving behind their little lair.

Frogs compose a symphony,
Croaking tunes quite merrily.
Underneath the twinkling sky,
The critters sing and laugh nearby.

Echoes bounce from branch to branch,
Nature joins in for a chance.
To share a laugh with every critter,
As stars above twinkle and glitter.

The Serpent's Satire

Slithering sly, a serpent grins,
With clever quips, he surely wins.
Tales of frogs and silly flies,
Brought forth laughter, oh what a surprise!

"Why jump so high?" the serpent asked,
"It's just the ground, it can be masked!"
Frogs croaked back, "We leap for fun,
While you just slide under the sun!"

The trees chuckled, leaves would sway,
As critters gathered, night and day.
With whispers shared in winks and giggles,
Life dripped down like sweetened twinkles.

So next time you hear hissing laughs,
Know it's the snake with his witty gaffs.
For in the grass where stories swirl,
Humor resides, a vibrant pearl.

Jests of the Jangling Jays

Jays in jackets, bright and bold,
Chattered tales of mischief told.
With feathers fluffed in vibrant glee,
They swoop and dive, wild and free.

"Look out below!" a jay would call,
As acorns dropped for fun, not fall.
With squawks and chirps, they'd tease and jest,
Bringing laughter on nature's quest.

Upon the branches, they would perch,
Planning pranks with a playful lurch.
"Who stole my berry?" one would cry,
While rolling back with a winked eye.

In a chorus of cackles bright,
They perform their antics, sheer delight.
For in their world, the jests will stay,
Echoing songs of a dazzling day.

Hidden Tales of the Harvest

Beneath the pumpkins, secrets grow,
Where shadows flicker, playfully so.
Rabbits plotting with wagging tails,
In the moonlight, they spin their trails.

"Let's paint the gourds!" one cheerfully said,
"Turn them to smiles, brighten the shed!"
With splashes of color, laughter spread,
As the field wore a vibrant thread.

Critters gather, their harvest feast,
Sharing bounty, the odd and the least.
With berries bobbing on every plate,
They feast and giggle, celebrating fate.

So as the sun dips, shadows dance,
Nature hums in a merry trance.
With tales so sweet, the harvest sings,
Of laughter shared, and joyful things.

Revelations Among Roots

Underneath the leafy spree,
A rabbit danced, wild and free.
He wore a hat far too grand,
With a carrot stick in hand.

The wise old owl hooted loud,
"Stop that nonsense! Be more proud!"
But the rabbit just twirled away,
Singing songs of the sunny day.

A squirrel rolled down a hill,
Chasing acorns with sheer will.
His friends laughed till they cried,
As he stumbled and then slide.

In the shade where shadows play,
The mischief never goes astray.
Whispers rustle in the breeze,
Joyful giggles 'neath the trees.

Folkloric Frolics of the Ferns

Beneath the fronds a tale unfurled,
A hedgehog twirled, his spikes all curled.
"I'm a prince!" he claimed with grace,
While the moths giggled in the space.

A party crickets threw that night,
With twinkling stars, a merry sight.
They danced on leaves to the moon's chant,
While a worm played his tiny chant.

The ants strutted, boots all polished,
Bragging dreams that all were varnished.
"Just watch us carry, can't you see?"
But one stumbled, "Oops! Not meant for me!"

Fern fronds swayed, a gentle cheer,
In this land of fun and maybe fear.
Where creatures spin tales in delight,
Turning whispers into the night.

The Glade's Grinning Secrets

In a glade where shadows play,
A fox dressed fine, without delay.
"I've got secrets," he would boast,
As the critters gathered, engrossed.

A bear with clumsy dance so grand,
Twisted, turning, lost his stand.
Laughter echoed, wild and free,
As he tumbled beneath the tree.

The mushrooms spoke, old tales they spun,
Of lost socks and misplaced fun.
Every whisper brought a cheer,
From the bunnies huddled near.

Strange puns floated through the air,
As critters competed with flair.
Each riddle spun a merry scene,
Joyful antics like a dream.

Echoes of Enchanted Antics

In the heart where mischief brews,
A porcupine shared the news.
"Let's have a ball!" he squeaked with glee,
As fireflies danced around a tree.

The raccoons came, their masks on tight,
Claiming treasures of the night.
But as they pranced with stolen toys,
They fell in mud, oh what noise!

The chatty sparrows chirped aloud,
"Join our feast! Come, gather 'round!"
With berries ripe and nuts to share,
Laughter rang through the vibrant air.

As dusk painted the sky with flair,
The echoes of joy hung in the air.
In every nook and cranny found,
The spirit of fun, profound!

The Owl's Observational Humor

In the night the wise owl hoots,
Joking of the clumsy brutes.
Squirrels fall from branches high,
Chasing tails as they fly by.

A rabbit slips on muddy ground,
While dancing, oh, where is he bound?
Owl chuckles from his lofty perch,
As laughter echoes from his church.

The fox rolls playfully in the leaves,
Wondering if humor deceives.
With each joke, the critters cheer,
While the owl winks, "You're all dear!"

So gather 'round, both meek and bold,
For the owl's tales never grow old!
In the night, where joys ignite,
Humor soars on wings of light.

Frolics of the Forest Floor

Amidst the ferns, the critters dance,
Each step a silly, joyful prance.
Badger trips on his own sheer might,
While sparrows giggle from their height.

The turtles race with all their might,
But end up snoozing in the light.
"Go on without me!" one did yawn,
While ants march on, from dusk till dawn.

A hedgehog boasts of speed and flair,
But rolls away without a care.
The forest floor is a stage so grand,
Where funny tales forever stand.

So frolic forth, you merry crew,
In the wild where silliness is true.
With laughter shared and joy in store,
Let the antics burst, forevermore!

Chronicles of the Crescent Moon

Beneath the moon, the shadows play,
As creatures gather for the fray.
The raccoon juggles nuts with ease,
While the owls hoot, "He aims to please!"

A wise old crow with a witty quip,
Sips from a cup, takes a dip.
"Who needs a party? Come see my show!"
As the marsh frogs join in, row by row.

With laughter bright, they share a tale,
Of mischief done without a trail.
The moonlight glows on furry friends,
As silly stories never end.

In this grand dance under the sky,
With chuckles light, we soar and fly.
As nocturnal laughter fills the night,
The crescent moon beams with delight.

Shenanigans in the Shaded Glade

In the glade, beneath the trees,
A band of friends brings silly tease.
Chasing tails and swinging low,
While giggling whispers start to flow.

Thechipmunks race, their cheeks so full,
While bear snores loud, a furry lull.
Squirrels plot, with mischief clear,
"Let's make the sleeping bear our deer!"

With acorns flying, all in jest,
The bear awakes, quite unimpressed.
But seeing smiles, his frown does fade,
As laughter echoes in the glade.

So come, dear critters, join the fun,
Under the shade, let's play and run.
For in this spot, both bright and bold,
The sweetest tales of joy unfold.

Mythical Musings of the Green

In the glen where shadows dance,
A squirrel juggles all by chance.
With acorns tossed in playful spouts,
He teases the birds with silly clouts.

The wise old owl, with glasses askew,
Sips on tea, as the crew pursue.
A fox in socks, he prances around,
While rabbits giggle without a sound.

A deer shares jokes, but can't keep straight,
About a hare who's just too late.
The laughter echoes, wild and free,
In this wood of whimsy, joy's decree.

So come and join these antics bright,
Where every day's a sheer delight.
In the realm of tricksters, sly and bold,
Their tales of mirth are sweetly told.

Folktales in Ferns

Beneath the fronds, a tale unfolds,
Of a turtle slow, but laughs untold.
He raced a hare, with vigor strong,
And sang a tune all the way long.

The frogs gave cheers, a chorus loud,
While crickets chirped, they formed a crowd.
Each twist and turn a jest to spin,
As the turtle wore a cheeky grin.

The wind whispered secrets, soft and sly,
Of creatures quipping as they passed by.
In ferns so lush, the stories bloom,
With laughter lingering, dispelling gloom.

Each corner turned brings more to see,
In the light of leaf, such jubilee.
With every step, the rhythm flows,
In the land where hilarity grows.

Laughter in Leafy Retreats

In shady nooks where sunlight dapples,
A raccoon plans his grand mere scrambles.
With sticky paws and mischief pure,
He'll swipe some snacks; that's for sure!

A chipmunk on a tiny stage,
Recites a poem that's quite the rage.
His tiny tophat cocked just right,
Makes every critter laugh with delight.

The hedgehog guest stars, a lovely sight,
He rolls around, much to their delight.
The laughter swells like a bubbling brook,
In leafy retreats, each nook a book.

So gather close and hear the cheer,
From all the critters you hold dear.
In laughter's arms, let worries cease,
As joy unfurls, a sweet release.

The Prankster's Path

Along the trail where laughter blooms,
A fox concocts his clever tunes.
He hides and waits with bated breath,
For a rabbit hopping, quick as death.

With a splash of paint on the rabbit's tail,
The forest bursts with giggles frail.
Oh, how they squeal and dance around,
As pranks ignite and joy is found!

The bear grumbles, not much amused,
But joins the fun, feeling quite enthused.
With honey pots and sticky feet,
He flips and rolls, a sight so sweet.

The path of jest leads all astray,
In guffaws that light the day.
So follow the laughter, step with glee,
In this world where we're all carefree.

Secrets in the Thicket

In a thicket thick with secrets,
Squirrels plot with glee,
Chatty owls tell tall tales,
While the hedgehog sips his tea.

A rabbit wears a fez, quite proud,
He dances with a flair,
The flowers giggle at his steps,
As the breeze pulls at his hair.

Underneath the leafy greens,
A joke is passed along,
The fox with all the clever schemes,
Can't resist a playful song.

The laughter rolls like tumbleweed,
Through shadows and the light,
In the thicket filled with mischief,
Every day's a silly sight.

Where Creatures Spin Their Yarn

In the glen where stories grow,
The creatures weave their dreams,
A badger spins a yarn of woe,
While the rabbit brings the beans.

The hedgehog laughs through every tale,
He ticks off points with pride,
And every spin and silly trail,
Has a twist that cannot hide.

A wise old turtle drags his shoe,
While telling of his quest,
'I'll outrun you, my sprightly crew,'
He jested with a jest.

They cheered and clapped, a raucous band,
Of critters near and far,
As stories danced in the evening sand,
Beneath the twinkling star.

The Nutmeg Conspiracy

In the grove where nutmegs lie,
A rumor starts to brew,
The mice all plot, oh my oh my,
A spice heist for a stew!

The squirrel is the sneaky king,
With acorns for his crew,
His whiskers twitching, planning things,
While birds just watch askew.

'We'll steal the spice!' the chatter rose,
'We'll cook it into pie!'
But little do they know, and oh,
The chef was standing by.

With pots and pans and a silly grin,
That chef was planning too,
A nutmeg cake for them to win,
As laughter filled the stew.

Laughter among the Branches

Among the branches, giggles float,
A parrot tells a tale,
While monkeys swing with glee and gloat,
As nutty winds prevail.

A wise old owl spins bits of fun,
With puns that twist and turn,
'One must not chase the shiny sun,'
He hoots, 'or you'll just burn!'

The branches sway in merry dance,
With critters large and small,
Each adds a quip, a quirky chance,
To make the laughter sprawl.

So if you roam where echoes thrive,
In laughter's warm embrace,
You'll find the trees are truly alive,
In this joyful, jolly place.

Legends of the Laughing Leaves

Once a tree wore a silly hat,
Breezes laughed, oh what of that!
Owls hooted jokes from high above,
While squirrels danced in the branch of love.

Sunbeams tickled the bark so bright,
Each giggle spread like pure delight.
Tails twitched, a chorus of cheer,
Nature's jesters we hold so dear.

Quips in the Quagmire

In muddy pits, frogs shared a tale,
With each jump, they'd wiggle and flail.
A turtle snickered, slow but wise,
As bubbles burst, a joke did rise.

Mice in boots pranced through the muck,
With cheesy puns, they struck their luck.
Every splash brought snorts and peeps,
In the mire, laughter never sleeps.

The Secret Society of Squirrels

Nuts in hand, the squirrels convene,
In shadows cast, their plans unseen.
With twitching tails, they craft a scheme,
To steal the acorns, a nutty dream.

Chirps of laughter fill the air,
As they plot with utmost care.
One tells tales of a daring heist,
While others squeak, 'Be bold, be nice!'

Eclectic Echoes of Enchantment

A chorus of critters, each with a song,
Gathered 'round where the flowers throng.
Bees buzzed puns, a musical spree,
While daisies swayed in jubilee.

A clover giggled, a giggle so sweet,
With every note, a tap of the feet.
The magic of mirth filled every nook,
As laughter danced like a playful brook.

Dances in the Dappled Light

In the shade where shadows play,
Squirrels dance and shout hooray.
A rabbit twirls in bright green socks,
While clumsy owls miscount their clocks.

The sunlight giggles through the leaves,
As hedgehogs plot some grand pranks, please!
A raccoon slips on a banana peel,
And lifts the crowd with his silly squeal.

Through the branches laughter flows,
As chipmunks wear the silliest clothes.
Frogs croak tunes that make them sway,
In the dappled light, they love to play.

So join the fun where giggles bloom,
Where every critter finds their room.
With mischief thick as honeyed sweet,
In the dance of life, all critters meet.

The Folktale's Green Embrace

Once upon a mossy knoll,
A wise old tree began to roll.
With stories trapped in every ring,
And squirrels listening, it starts to sing.

A badger dressed in finest rags,
Tells awfully funny tales of jags.
While fireflies flicker in sheer delight,
As shadows dance beneath the night.

The fox, he prances with wily flair,
While frogs leap past without a care.
With giggles echoing in the air,
These tales of green, a joyous affair!

And as the moonlight paints the scene,
Nighttime creatures share their keen.
With every yarn that finds its trace,
The woods alive in joyful grace.

Parables of Pine and Prowess

Among the pines, a tale unfolds,
Of daring deeds and antics bold.
With porcupines armed with tiny swords,
And critters jousting in wild hordes.

The woodpecker taps a funny beat,
As beavers march with growing fleet.
Each creature boasts of wins and losses,
While the wise owl calculates their bosses.

A turtle with a swagger so grand,
Challenges anyone to take a stand.
With a laugh and a wink, he starts to strut,
And leaves them all in quite a rut.

So gather round, dear woodland kin,
To share your tales, let the laughter begin.
For in the woods where stories blend,
The fun is endless, around each bend.

The Jester of the Woodlands

A merry jester roams the glade,
In mismatched shoes and bright beret.
He juggles acorns with great flair,
And sends the raccoons into despair.

With every trick, he lights the scene,
As butterflies join in the routine.
A fox rolls over, laughs till he squeaks,
While hedgehogs snort with playful beaks.

When the moon rises, he tells a joke,
About a lost chicken searching for smoke.
The trees shake gently, as laughter spreads,
Even the quietest bunnies dread!

So if you wander where shadows blend,
Seek the jester, your new best friend.
For in the wild where joy ignites,
Laughter dances on starry nights.

The Goblin's Grin

In shadows deep, the goblin prances,
With mischief born from wild glances.
He swipes a hat, he steals a shoe,
And giggles loud, oh what a view!

He dances 'round the sleeping deer,
And whispers jokes that only they hear.
The squirrel snickers, the owl rolls eyes,
As goblin tricks lead to big surprise!

He paints the trees in colors bright,
With laughter echoing into the night.
"Come join my fun, don't be so grim!"
But who would trust that goblin's whim?

When dawn arrives, he's off like smoke,
Leaving behind a minstrel's joke.
So if you wander, heed this spin:
Always laugh in the goblin's grin!

Treetop Tattle

The birds in branches share their tales,
Of breezy flights and windy gales.
A woodpecker knocks out beats so sweet,
As gossip travels on tiny feet.

The rabbit hops by, ears a-flop,
And claims the fox can't dance, just stop!
But fox, so sly, with a wink and a twist,
Proves that even he can't be missed.

The chatty mice in dappled shade,
Weave stories bold, though truth may fade.
"Oh, didn't you hear? The badger sings!
Every dusk, he flaunts such wild things!"

They laugh and chuckle 'neath the sun's glow,
Where secrets sprout and tall tales grow.
In the canopy high, beneath the skies,
Treetop tattle never dies!

Carols of the Chattering Critters

In twilight's glow, the critters conspire,
With tunes that twinkle like a campfire.
The frogs declare, "We lead the band!"
As crickets chirp, their legs expand.

A turtle hums, though moving slow,
While mice play keys with a nifty show.
The hedgehogs sway, all prickly and fine,
Singing of dreams with a punch of wine!

In harmony, the raccoons serenade,
With spoons for drums, a wild parade.
A chattering choir, so wild and free,
They sing of laughs beneath the tree.

When morning breaks, the notes still soar,
With echoes bright and spirits galore.
These merry critters craft their song,
In the heart of night, where they all belong!

Arcane Antics in the Arbor

Within the boughs where shadows twitch,
A wizard's spell goes slightly amiss.
A flick of wand, a puff of smoke,
And all the squirrels start to croak!

The spells take flight on wings of wit,
As pixies dance, refusing to sit.
"Keep your eyes peeled," the wizard calls,
"For in this woods, chaos befalls!"

The trees start wobbling, the bunnies bounce,
As bees in hats begin to prounce.
With laughter bubbling, spells miscast,
This woodland party is a blast!

And when the moon hangs big and round,
The arcane antics shake the ground.
So if you wander near the glade,
Join the fun where magic is made!

Jests on the Juniper

In the shade of the juniper's sway,
A squirrel proclaimed it was his birthday play.
With nuts as his cake, he danced all around,
While birds sang and chuckled, their joy was profound.

A rabbit joined in, sporting a hat,
He juggled some acorns and fell with a splat.
The laughter grew louder as friends gathered near,
Nature's own laughter, a sweet serenade here.

A hedgehog then stood, with a grin ear to ear,
"I've got a great joke, come lend me your ear!"
He spoke of a thorn that tried to be bold,
But tickled a badger, who lost it, behold!

The juniper rustled, sharing secrets galore,
As creatures recounted tales of yore.
With giggles and snorts, the woodland did cheer,
The heart of the woodland, so light and so clear.

Willow's Whispered Wit

Willow the wise had much to impart,
With leaves in her hair, she captured each heart.
She told of a frog, who tried to sing high,
But croaked out a note that just made others cry.

Her laughter would ripple through branches and skies,
As crickets would chirp their comedic replies.
A turtle came by, with a tale of regret,
He'd raced with a hare, but lost his best bet.

With a twinkle of twilight, the joke took a turn,
Willow leaned close, "Let's see how you learn!
A spider who weaved a most stylish ensemble,
Got caught in her web—oh, what a fine scramble!"

The fireflies joined in with a glimmering gleam,
Illuminating laughter, like a bright, shared dream.
In the cool of the night, where mirth took its lead,
Willow's wise whispers planted each silly seed.

Tales from the Tangled Roots

Among tangled roots where the laughter takes flight,
A raccoon spun a yarn to the stars of the night.
He wore a small mask, played the role of a thief,
Stealing the hearts of all, oh what a relief!

The hedgehogs in circles, they giggled and squeaked,
As his stories became increasingly cheeked.
A fox chimed in, with a grin wide and bold,
"I once stole a berry, but it turned out to mold!"

The chatter grew louder—what nonsense they shared,
Of things that to most would seem wildly impaired.
A owl made faces, his wisdom was lost,
"Tell me again how you guys paid the cost!"

With each twist of the tale, from roots to the sky,
They painted the night with laughter on high.
In a world full of whimsy, they danced with delight,
Where funny fables took flight in the night.

The Mischievous Moss

Moss met the moon, under soft silver beams,
He whispered of pranks that emerged from his dreams.
About a sly mouse who nibbled on cheese,
But found it was paper—oh, what a tease!

With each silly tale, the night came alive,
The laughter and giggles began to derive.
A wise old lizard, in search of a friend,
Declared he could dance—then straight tripped on a bend!

He landed near moss, who chuckled in fits,
"Next time try some twirls, not just silly skits!"
A beetle then joined, with a riddle to share,
"What's black and makes everyone stop and stare?"

They all held their breath, anticipation grew,
"A crow who stole socks, now isn't that true?"
With laughter erupting, the moss swayed with glee,
In the glow of the night, where jesting runs free.

www.ingramcontent.com/pod-product-compliance
Lightning Source LLC
Chambersburg PA
CBHW071817160426
43209CB00003B/124